Let's Talk Abo

PLAYING WITH OTHERS

AN EARLY SOCIAL SKILLS BOOK

Written by Joy Berry   **Illustrated by Roey**

GOLD STAR PUBLISHING™

Hello, my name is Tabby.
I'd like to tell you a story
about my friend, Annie.

Like Annie, you might not like it when people will not play with you.

When people will not
play with you, you might
feel left out, rejected, sad,
and lonely.

6

Sometimes people will not play with you because they are too busy to play.

Try not to bother a person who is too busy to play.
Do these things instead:

- Make a plan to play together at a time when the person is not busy.
- Wait for that time.
- Do not bother the person while you wait.

Can you play with me when you've finished washing the car?

Now, let's leave him alone so he can finish washing the car.

13

Sometimes people will not play with you because they would rather do something else.

14

15

Begging people to play
with you, when they prefer
doing something else,
might frustrate them.
If people become
frustrated with you,
you might feel bad.

Your begging is
only annoying
him.

17

Avoid begging a person to play with you when the person would rather do something else. Do these things instead:

- Think about doing whatever activity the other person prefers to do.
- Talk to the person about it.
- Do something else if the other person does not want to include you in the activity.

Now, that's more like it!

19

Sometimes people will not
play with you because
they do not like the way
you behave around them.

21

People will most likely want to play with you when you treat them the way you want to be treated.

22

23

One way to treat other people the way you want to be treated is to be respectful.

- Avoid doing anything that would hurt others.
- Avoid doing anything that would damage someone else's things.
- Avoid being bossy.

25

A second way to treat other people the way you want to be treated is to be fair.

- Avoid insisting on having the best or most of everything.
- Take turns with others when deciding what to do.
- Avoid cheating.

You're not being very fair.

27

A third way to treat other people the way you want to be treated is to be kind.

- Share your things with others.
- Say and do things to make others feel better.

29

Sometimes you might not be able to get anyone to play with you. That is when you need to entertain yourself. It is important that you have permission to do whatever you choose to do.

31

If you want people to play with you, you need to be considerate and treat others the way you would like to be treated.